70 Rice and Grain Recipes for Home

By: Kelly Johnson

Table of Contents

Breakfast:
- Fluffy Pancakes with Whipped Cream
- Classic French Toast with Maple Syrup
- Creamy Yogurt Parfait with Fresh Berries and Granola
- Cheesy Spinach and Feta Omelette
- Cream Cheese Stuffed Bagels with Smoked Salmon

Appetizers:
- Baked Brie with Honey and Walnuts
- Caprese Skewers with Mozzarella, Tomatoes, and Basil
- Spinach and Artichoke Dip with Cream Cheese
- Gourmet Cheese and Charcuterie Board
- Creamy Garlic Parmesan Shrimp

Soups:
- Creamy Tomato Basil Soup with Mascarpone
- Broccoli Cheddar Soup
- Potato Leek Soup with Sour Cream
- Creamy Mushroom Soup with Gruyère Croutons
- Corn Chowder with Cheddar and Bacon

Salads:
- Caesar Salad with Homemade Dressing and Parmesan Crisps
- Creamy Coleslaw with Buttermilk Dressing
- Greek Salad with Feta and Kalamata Olives
- Avocado and Goat Cheese Salad with Balsamic Vinaigrette
- Waldorf Salad with Blue Cheese Dressing

Main Courses:
- Creamy Alfredo Pasta with Grilled Chicken
- Four-Cheese Lasagna
- Beef Stroganoff with Sour Cream
- Spinach and Ricotta Stuffed Chicken Breast
- Creamy Shrimp Scampi over Linguine

Vegetarian Options:
- Three-Cheese Spinach and Mushroom Stuffed Peppers
- Eggplant Parmesan with Mozzarella
- Creamy Pesto Pasta Primavera
- Cheesy Zucchini and Tomato Gratin

Side Dishes:
- Spinach and Ricotta Stuffed Shells
- Creamy Mashed Potatoes with Butter and Cream
- Grilled Asparagus with Parmesan Cheese
- Creamed Spinach with Nutmeg
- Macaroni and Cheese with a Crispy Bread Crumb Topping
- Scalloped Potatoes with Gruyère and Thyme

Breads and Rolls:
- Cheesy Garlic Breadsticks
- Cheddar and Herb Biscuits
- Cream Cheese Danish Pastry
- Gouda and Chive Scones
- Feta and Sun-Dried Tomato Pull-Apart Bread

Breakfast:
Fluffy Pancakes with Whipped Cream

Ingredients:

- 1 cup all-purpose flour
- 2 tablespoons sugar
- 1 teaspoon baking powder
- 1/2 teaspoon baking soda
- 1/4 teaspoon salt
- 3/4 cup buttermilk
- 1/4 cup milk
- 1 large egg
- 2 tablespoons unsalted butter, melted
- 1 teaspoon vanilla extract

For serving:

- Whipped cream
- Maple syrup
- Fresh berries (optional)

Instructions:

Prepare the Dry Ingredients:

In a large mixing bowl, whisk together the flour, sugar, baking powder, baking soda, and salt. Ensure that the dry ingredients are well combined.

Combine Wet Ingredients:

In a separate bowl, whisk together the buttermilk, milk, egg, melted butter, and vanilla extract.

Mix Wet and Dry Ingredients:

Pour the wet ingredients into the dry ingredients. Gently stir until just combined. Be careful not to overmix; a few lumps are okay. Let the batter rest for a few minutes.

Preheat the Griddle or Pan:

Preheat a griddle or non-stick pan over medium heat. Lightly grease it with butter or cooking spray.

Cook the Pancakes:

Pour 1/4 cup of batter onto the hot griddle for each pancake. Cook until bubbles form on the surface, then flip and cook until the other side is golden brown. Repeat until all the batter is used.

Serve:

Stack the pancakes on a plate. Top with a dollop of whipped cream and fresh berries if desired. Drizzle with maple syrup.

Enjoy:

Serve the fluffy pancakes warm and enjoy the delightful combination of light, airy pancakes with the sweetness of whipped cream and the richness of maple syrup.

These fluffy pancakes with whipped cream make for a delicious and indulgent breakfast or brunch treat that will surely delight your taste buds.

Classic French Toast with Maple Syrup

Ingredients:

- 4 slices of thick-cut bread (such as brioche or challah)
- 2 large eggs
- 1/2 cup whole milk
- 1 teaspoon vanilla extract
- 1/2 teaspoon ground cinnamon
- Pinch of salt
- Butter, for cooking
- Maple syrup, for serving
- Powdered sugar and fresh berries (optional, for garnish)

Instructions:

Preheat the Griddle or Pan:

Preheat a griddle or non-stick pan over medium heat.

Prepare the Batter:

In a shallow dish, whisk together the eggs, milk, vanilla extract, ground cinnamon, and a pinch of salt until well combined.

Soak the Bread:

Dip each slice of bread into the egg mixture, ensuring both sides are coated. Allow excess to drip off.

Cook the French Toast:

Add a small amount of butter to the preheated griddle or pan. Place the soaked bread slices onto the cooking surface. Cook for 2-3 minutes on each side or until golden brown and cooked through.

Keep Warm:

If making multiple batches, you can keep the cooked French toast warm in a preheated oven (around 200°F or 93°C) while you cook the rest.

Serve:

Place the cooked French toast on a plate. Drizzle with maple syrup and, if desired, sprinkle with powdered sugar. Add fresh berries for a burst of color and flavor.

Enjoy:

Serve the classic French toast warm and enjoy the perfect combination of crispy edges, soft centers, and the sweetness of maple syrup.

This classic French toast recipe is simple yet indulgent, making it a delightful breakfast or brunch option for any occasion. Customize it with your favorite toppings and savor the comforting flavors of this timeless dish.

Creamy Yogurt Parfait with Fresh Berries and Granola

Ingredients:

- 1 cup Greek yogurt (plain or vanilla)
- 2 tablespoons honey or maple syrup
- 1 teaspoon vanilla extract
- 1 cup mixed fresh berries (strawberries, blueberries, raspberries)
- 1/2 cup granola (homemade or store-bought)
- Fresh mint leaves for garnish (optional)

Instructions:

Prepare the Yogurt Mixture:

In a bowl, combine the Greek yogurt, honey or maple syrup, and vanilla extract. Mix well until the sweetener is evenly incorporated into the yogurt.

Layer the Parfait:

Take a glass or a serving dish. Begin by adding a layer of the sweetened yogurt to the bottom.

Add Fresh Berries:

Add a layer of mixed fresh berries on top of the yogurt. You can use a combination of sliced strawberries, blueberries, and raspberries.

Sprinkle Granola:

Sprinkle a layer of granola over the berries. This adds a delightful crunch and complements the creaminess of the yogurt.

Repeat Layers:

Repeat the layers until you reach the top of the glass or dish. Finish with a final layer of yogurt and top with a few extra berries and a sprinkle of granola.

Garnish:

If desired, garnish the top with fresh mint leaves for a burst of freshness.

Serve:

Serve the creamy yogurt parfait immediately, or refrigerate for a short time to chill before serving.

Enjoy:

Grab a spoon and enjoy the delightful combination of creamy yogurt, sweet berries, and crunchy granola in each mouthful.

This yogurt parfait is not only visually appealing but also a wholesome and satisfying treat for breakfast, a snack, or even a light dessert. Feel free to customize the parfait with your favorite fruits, nuts, or seeds for added variety and nutrition.

Cheesy Spinach and Feta Omelette

Ingredients:

- 3 large eggs
- Salt and pepper to taste
- 1 tablespoon butter or olive oil
- 1 cup fresh spinach, chopped
- 1/4 cup crumbled feta cheese
- 2 tablespoons grated Parmesan cheese
- 1 tablespoon fresh herbs (such as parsley or chives), chopped (optional)

Instructions:

Prepare the Eggs:

Crack the eggs into a bowl, add a pinch of salt and pepper, and whisk them until well combined.

Saute Spinach:

Heat butter or olive oil in a non-stick skillet over medium heat. Add the chopped spinach and sauté for 1-2 minutes until wilted.

Pour in the Eggs:

Pour the whisked eggs over the sautéed spinach in the skillet. Swirl the pan to ensure the eggs cover the entire surface.

Add Feta Cheese:

Sprinkle crumbled feta cheese evenly over one half of the omelette.

Fold and Cook:

Once the edges of the omelette start setting, use a spatula to gently fold the omelette in half, covering the side with the feta cheese.

Melt Parmesan Cheese:

Sprinkle grated Parmesan cheese over the top of the folded omelette. Allow it to melt for about 30 seconds.

Cook until Set:

Continue cooking the omelette for another 1-2 minutes or until the eggs are fully set but still moist.

Garnish and Serve:

Slide the omelette onto a plate. Garnish with fresh herbs if desired.

Enjoy:

Serve the cheesy spinach and feta omelette hot, and savor the combination of creamy feta, sautéed spinach, and fluffy eggs.

This cheesy spinach and feta omelette is a quick and nutritious breakfast option that provides a perfect balance of flavors. Customize it by adding tomatoes, mushrooms, or bell peppers for an extra burst of freshness and color.

Cream Cheese Stuffed Bagels with Smoked Salmon

Ingredients:

For the Bagels:

- 4 plain bagels, sliced in half
- 1 cup whipped cream cheese
- 2 tablespoons fresh chives, chopped
- Salt and black pepper to taste

For the Smoked Salmon Topping:

- 8 slices smoked salmon
- Red onion, thinly sliced (optional)
- Capers, for garnish
- Fresh dill, for garnish
- Lemon wedges, for serving

Instructions:

Prepare the Bagels:

Preheat the oven to 350°F (175°C). Place the bagel halves on a baking sheet.

Whip the Cream Cheese:

In a bowl, combine the whipped cream cheese, chopped chives, salt, and black pepper. Mix well.

Spread Cream Cheese:

Spread a generous layer of the whipped cream cheese mixture on each bagel half.

Assemble the Bagels:

Place a slice of smoked salmon on the bottom half of each bagel. Optionally, add thinly sliced red onion for an extra kick.

Complete the Toppings:

Garnish each bagel with capers and fresh dill. The capers add a tangy kick, and the dill complements the flavors of the smoked salmon.

Bake in the Oven:

Place the prepared bagels in the preheated oven and bake for about 5-7 minutes, or until the cream cheese is slightly softened and the bagels are warmed.

Serve:

Remove the bagels from the oven and assemble them by placing the top half over the smoked salmon. Arrange the bagels on a serving platter.

Garnish and Serve:

Garnish the platter with additional fresh dill and lemon wedges on the side. The lemon wedges can be squeezed over the smoked salmon for extra brightness.

Enjoy:

Serve the cream cheese stuffed bagels with smoked salmon immediately, and enjoy this classic and delicious combination!

This delightful recipe combines the richness of whipped cream cheese, the smoky flavor of salmon, and the freshness of herbs for a perfect breakfast or brunch treat. It's a classic bagel experience elevated to gourmet heights.

Appetizers:
Baked Brie with Honey and Walnuts

Ingredients:

- 1 wheel of Brie cheese (8-10 ounces)
- 1/3 cup walnuts, chopped
- 2 tablespoons honey
- 1 tablespoon fresh rosemary, finely chopped
- Crackers or baguette slices, for serving

Instructions:

Preheat the Oven:

    Preheat your oven to 350°F (175°C).

Prepare the Brie:

    Place the wheel of Brie on a baking sheet lined with parchment paper.

Score the Brie:

    Use a sharp knife to make a few shallow cuts on the top rind of the Brie. This helps the cheese absorb the flavors.

Top with Walnuts:

    Sprinkle the chopped walnuts evenly over the top of the Brie.

Drizzle with Honey:

    Drizzle the honey over the walnuts and Brie, ensuring it's spread evenly.

Add Rosemary:

    Sprinkle the finely chopped fresh rosemary on top of the honey and walnuts.

Bake in the Oven:

Place the baking sheet with the Brie in the preheated oven. Bake for about 10-12 minutes or until the Brie is soft and gooey.

Serve:

Carefully transfer the baked Brie to a serving platter. Allow it to cool for a few minutes before serving.

Garnish (Optional):

If desired, garnish with additional fresh rosemary and a drizzle of honey for presentation.

Serve with Crackers or Baguette:

Arrange crackers or baguette slices around the baked Brie for easy dipping.

Enjoy:

Serve the baked Brie with honey and walnuts immediately while it's warm and gooey. Encourage guests to scoop up the melted cheese with crackers or slices of baguette.

This Baked Brie with Honey and Walnuts is an elegant and crowd-pleasing appetizer, perfect for gatherings or as a delicious start to a special meal. The combination of creamy Brie, sweet honey, and crunchy walnuts creates a delightful harmony of flavors and textures.

Caprese Skewers with Mozzarella, Tomatoes, and Basil

Ingredients:

- Fresh mozzarella balls (bocconcini), about 20 pieces
- Cherry or grape tomatoes, about 20 pieces
- Fresh basil leaves, about 20 leaves
- Balsamic glaze (store-bought or homemade)
- Extra-virgin olive oil
- Salt and pepper to taste
- Wooden or metal skewers

Instructions:

Prepare Ingredients:

Wash and dry the cherry or grape tomatoes. Drain the fresh mozzarella balls if they're in liquid. Ensure the basil leaves are clean and dry.

Assemble Skewers:

Take a skewer and thread one mozzarella ball, one basil leaf (folded if large), and one tomato onto it. Repeat until each skewer is filled with a combination of mozzarella, basil, and tomato.

Arrange Skewers:

Lay the assembled Caprese skewers on a serving platter.

Drizzle with Olive Oil:

Drizzle the skewers with extra-virgin olive oil. Ensure each skewer gets a light coating.

Season with Salt and Pepper:

Season the skewers with a pinch of salt and pepper to enhance the flavors.

Drizzle with Balsamic Glaze:

Drizzle the Caprese skewers with balsamic glaze for a sweet and tangy finish. If you don't have balsamic glaze, you can reduce balsamic vinegar in a saucepan until it thickens.

Serve:

Arrange the Caprese skewers on a platter and serve them immediately.

Enjoy:

These Caprese skewers are perfect for a light appetizer or a refreshing addition to a summer party. The combination of fresh mozzarella, ripe tomatoes, and aromatic basil, drizzled with balsamic glaze, creates a classic and delightful flavor profile.

Feel free to customize by adding a sprinkle of sea salt, a dash of black pepper, or a touch of fresh herbs for an extra burst of flavor.

Spinach and Artichoke Dip with Cream Cheese

Ingredients:

- 1 (10-ounce) package frozen chopped spinach, thawed and drained
- 1 (14-ounce) can artichoke hearts, drained and chopped
- 1 cup cream cheese, softened
- 1/2 cup mayonnaise
- 1/2 cup sour cream
- 1 cup grated Parmesan cheese
- 1 cup shredded mozzarella cheese
- 2 cloves garlic, minced
- 1/2 teaspoon onion powder
- 1/2 teaspoon garlic powder
- 1/2 teaspoon crushed red pepper flakes (optional, for a hint of heat)
- Salt and black pepper to taste

For Serving:

- Tortilla chips, baguette slices, or vegetable sticks

Instructions:

Preheat the Oven:

   Preheat your oven to 375°F (190°C).

Prepare Spinach and Artichokes:

   Ensure the frozen chopped spinach is thawed and well-drained. Chop the drained artichoke hearts into smaller pieces.

Mix Cream Cheese Base:

   In a mixing bowl, combine the softened cream cheese, mayonnaise, and sour cream. Mix until smooth and well combined.

Add Remaining Ingredients:

Add the drained spinach, chopped artichokes, grated Parmesan cheese, shredded mozzarella cheese, minced garlic, onion powder, garlic powder, and crushed red pepper flakes (if using) to the cream cheese mixture. Mix well to incorporate all the ingredients.

Season and Adjust:

Season the mixture with salt and black pepper to taste. Adjust the seasonings as needed.

Transfer to Baking Dish:

Transfer the mixture to a baking dish, spreading it out evenly.

Bake in the Oven:

Bake in the preheated oven for approximately 25-30 minutes, or until the dip is hot, bubbly, and the top is golden brown.

Serve:

Remove the dip from the oven and let it cool for a few minutes before serving.

Enjoy:

Serve the spinach and artichoke dip with cream cheese alongside tortilla chips, baguette slices, or vegetable sticks. Enjoy the creamy, cheesy goodness!

This Spinach and Artichoke Dip with Cream Cheese is a classic crowd-pleaser, perfect for parties, game nights, or any gathering. The combination of creamy textures, savory flavors, and the hint of spinach and artichoke make it an irresistible appetizer.

Gourmet Cheese and Charcuterie Board

Cheeses:

    Brie: Creamy and mild.
    Gouda: Aged for a rich, nutty flavor.
    Blue Cheese: Sharp and pungent.
    Manchego: Firm sheep's milk cheese with a nutty taste.
    Goat Cheese (Chevre): Tangy and spreadable.
    Camembert: Soft, creamy, and earthy.

Charcuterie:

    Prosciutto: Thinly sliced, dry-cured ham.
    Salami: A variety of cured meats such as Genoa, soppressata, or chorizo.
    Chorizo: Spanish sausage with smoky and spicy notes.
    Pâté: Smooth chicken liver or mushroom pâté.
    Capicola: Italian cold cut with a slightly spicy flavor.

Accompaniments:

    Crackers and Bread:
- Artisanal crackers
- Baguette slices
- Fig or olive bread

    Fresh and Dried Fruits:
- Grapes
- Apple slices
- Figs or dates
- Dried apricots

    Nuts:
- Marcona almonds
- Candied walnuts or pecans

    Spreads and Condiments:
- Whole grain mustard
- Honey or fig jam
- Balsamic reduction
- Olive tapenade

    Pickles and Olives:

- Cornichons
- Mixed olives (green and black)
- Pickled onions

Extras:
- Dark chocolate squares
- Edible flowers for decoration
- Fresh herbs (rosemary, thyme) for garnish

Assembly Tips:

Placement: Arrange cheeses and charcuterie in a balanced manner, ensuring a variety of textures and flavors in each section.
Spacing: Provide enough space between items to allow easy access without overcrowding.
Artistic Touch: Consider the visual appeal by placing items in a visually appealing pattern. Mix colors, shapes, and sizes for an attractive presentation.
Labeling: Place small signs or labels to identify each cheese and charcuterie item.
Temperature: Serve cheeses at room temperature for the best flavor. Take them out of the refrigerator at least 30 minutes before serving.
Pairing: Encourage guests to pair different cheeses with specific accompaniments for a delightful tasting experience.

A well-curated Gourmet Cheese and Charcuterie Board provides a sophisticated and diverse array of flavors, making it an excellent centerpiece for social gatherings and celebrations.

Creamy Garlic Parmesan Shrimp

Ingredients:

- 1 pound large shrimp, peeled and deveined
- 3 tablespoons butter, divided
- 4 cloves garlic, minced
- 1 cup heavy cream
- 1 cup grated Parmesan cheese
- Salt and black pepper to taste
- 1 teaspoon paprika
- Fresh parsley, chopped, for garnish
- Lemon wedges, for serving
- Cooked pasta or crusty bread, for serving (optional)

Instructions:

Prepare Shrimp:

Pat the shrimp dry with paper towels. Season with salt, black pepper, and paprika.

Cook Shrimp:

In a large skillet, heat 2 tablespoons of butter over medium-high heat. Add the seasoned shrimp and cook for 2-3 minutes per side or until they turn pink and opaque. Remove shrimp from the skillet and set aside.

Saute Garlic:

In the same skillet, add the remaining tablespoon of butter. Add minced garlic and sauté for about 1 minute until fragrant.

Make Cream Sauce:

Pour in the heavy cream, stirring continuously. Bring the cream to a simmer, then reduce heat to low.

Add Parmesan:

Gradually whisk in the grated Parmesan cheese until the sauce is smooth and creamy.

Combine Shrimp and Sauce:

Return the cooked shrimp to the skillet, coating them with the creamy garlic Parmesan sauce. Simmer for an additional 2-3 minutes until the shrimp are heated through.

Season and Garnish:

Taste the sauce and adjust the seasoning with salt and black pepper as needed. Stir in chopped fresh parsley for added flavor and color.

Serve:

Spoon the creamy garlic Parmesan shrimp over cooked pasta or serve with crusty bread. Garnish with additional parsley and lemon wedges on the side.

Enjoy:

Serve immediately, and enjoy this decadent and flavorful creamy garlic Parmesan shrimp dish.

This creamy garlic Parmesan shrimp recipe is a delightful combination of succulent shrimp coated in a rich, velvety sauce. It's perfect over pasta or with a side of crusty bread for soaking up the delicious sauce.

Soups:
Creamy Tomato Basil Soup with Mascarpone

Ingredients:

- 2 tablespoons olive oil
- 1 large onion, chopped
- 3 cloves garlic, minced
- 2 cans (28 ounces each) whole peeled tomatoes
- 1 can (14 ounces) crushed tomatoes
- 1 teaspoon dried basil
- 1 teaspoon dried oregano
- 1/2 teaspoon dried thyme
- 1/2 teaspoon red pepper flakes (optional, for a hint of heat)
- Salt and black pepper to taste
- 2 cups vegetable or chicken broth
- 1/2 cup mascarpone cheese
- 1/4 cup fresh basil, chopped, plus extra for garnish
- 1 cup heavy cream (optional, for extra creaminess)

Instructions:

Saute Aromatics:

In a large pot, heat olive oil over medium heat. Add chopped onions and sauté until they become translucent.

Add Garlic:

Add minced garlic to the onions and sauté for an additional 1-2 minutes until fragrant.

Tomato Base:

Pour in the whole peeled tomatoes, crushed tomatoes, dried basil, dried oregano, dried thyme, and red pepper flakes (if using). Break apart the whole tomatoes using a spoon.

Season:

Season the mixture with salt and black pepper to taste. Stir to combine.

Simmer:

Add the vegetable or chicken broth, then bring the soup to a simmer. Allow it to simmer for 15-20 minutes, allowing the flavors to meld.

Blend the Soup:

Use an immersion blender to carefully blend the soup until smooth. Alternatively, transfer the soup in batches to a blender and blend until smooth. Be cautious, as hot liquids can splatter.

Add Mascarpone and Fresh Basil:

Return the soup to low heat. Stir in the mascarpone cheese and chopped fresh basil. Continue to cook until the mascarpone is fully melted into the soup.

Optional: Add Heavy Cream

If you desire extra creaminess, stir in the heavy cream at this stage.

Adjust Seasoning:

Taste the soup and adjust the seasoning if necessary. You can add more salt, pepper, or herbs to suit your taste.

Serve:

Ladle the creamy tomato basil soup into bowls. Garnish with additional fresh basil.

Enjoy:

Serve this comforting soup hot, and enjoy the rich and creamy flavors.

This Creamy Tomato Basil Soup with Mascarpone is a luxurious and comforting dish perfect for a chilly day. The mascarpone adds a velvety texture and a touch of richness to the classic tomato basil soup.

Broccoli Cheddar Soup

Ingredients:

- 1/4 cup unsalted butter
- 1 onion, finely chopped
- 2 cloves garlic, minced
- 1/4 cup all-purpose flour
- 4 cups low-sodium chicken or vegetable broth
- 4 cups fresh broccoli florets, chopped
- 1 large carrot, peeled and grated
- 2 cups sharp cheddar cheese, shredded
- 1 cup whole milk
- 1 cup heavy cream
- Salt and black pepper to taste
- 1/4 teaspoon nutmeg (optional, for added warmth)
- Croutons or extra shredded cheddar for garnish (optional)

Instructions:

Saute Aromatics:

In a large pot, melt the butter over medium heat. Add chopped onions and sauté until softened, about 3-5 minutes. Add minced garlic and sauté for an additional 1-2 minutes until fragrant.

Make Roux:

Sprinkle the flour over the onion and garlic mixture, stirring constantly to create a roux. Cook for 2-3 minutes to eliminate the raw flour taste.

Add Broth:

Gradually whisk in the chicken or vegetable broth, ensuring there are no lumps. Bring the mixture to a simmer.

Add Broccoli and Carrot:

Add the chopped broccoli florets and grated carrot to the pot. Simmer for about 15 minutes or until the vegetables are tender.

Blend the Soup:

Use an immersion blender to blend the soup to your desired consistency. You can leave it slightly chunky or make it smoother.

Add Cheese and Milk:

Reduce the heat to low. Stir in the shredded cheddar cheese until melted. Pour in the whole milk and heavy cream, stirring continuously.

Season:

Season the soup with salt, black pepper, and nutmeg (if using). Adjust the seasoning to taste.

Simmer and Serve:

Allow the soup to simmer for an additional 10-15 minutes to let the flavors meld. Stir occasionally.

Garnish:

Optionally, garnish the soup with croutons or extra shredded cheddar before serving.

Serve:

Ladle the warm and creamy broccoli cheddar soup into bowls. Serve immediately.

Enjoy:

Enjoy this comforting and hearty soup as a delicious meal on its own or paired with crusty bread.

This Broccoli Cheddar Soup is a classic comfort food favorite, perfect for warming up on chilly days. The combination of rich cheddar cheese and wholesome broccoli makes for a satisfying and flavorful bowl of soup.

Potato Leek Soup with Sour Cream

Ingredients:

- 3 leeks, cleaned and sliced (white and light green parts only)
- 4 medium-sized potatoes, peeled and diced
- 2 tablespoons unsalted butter
- 1 tablespoon olive oil
- 2 cloves garlic, minced
- 6 cups vegetable or chicken broth
- 1 bay leaf
- Salt and black pepper to taste
- 1 cup sour cream
- Chives or fresh parsley, chopped (for garnish)

Instructions:

Prepare Leeks:

Clean the leeks thoroughly, slice them, and rinse to remove any dirt.

Saute Leeks and Garlic:

In a large pot, heat the butter and olive oil over medium heat. Add the sliced leeks and minced garlic. Saute for about 5-7 minutes until the leeks are softened.

Add Potatoes:

Add the diced potatoes to the pot and continue to sauté for an additional 3-5 minutes.

Pour in Broth:

Pour in the vegetable or chicken broth, and add the bay leaf. Bring the mixture to a boil.

Simmer:

Reduce the heat to low, cover the pot, and let the soup simmer for about 20-25 minutes or until the potatoes are tender.

Remove Bay Leaf:

Discard the bay leaf from the soup.

Blend Soup:

Use an immersion blender to blend the soup until smooth. Alternatively, transfer the soup in batches to a blender and blend until smooth. Be cautious, as hot liquids can splatter.

Add Sour Cream:

Stir in the sour cream, mixing until well incorporated.

Season:

Season the soup with salt and black pepper to taste. Adjust the seasoning according to your preference.

Serve:

Ladle the potato leek soup into bowls. Garnish with chopped chives or fresh parsley.

Enjoy:

Serve this creamy and comforting potato leek soup hot, and enjoy the rich and satisfying flavors.

This Potato Leek Soup with Sour Cream is a velvety, flavorful dish perfect for a comforting meal. The combination of leeks, potatoes, and sour cream creates a creamy and hearty soup that is sure to warm you up on a chilly day.

Creamy Mushroom Soup with Gruyère Croutons

Ingredients:

For the Soup:

- 2 tablespoons unsalted butter
- 1 onion, finely chopped
- 2 cloves garlic, minced
- 1 pound (about 500g) assorted mushrooms (such as cremini, shiitake, and button), sliced
- 4 cups vegetable or chicken broth
- 1 teaspoon thyme, chopped
- Salt and black pepper to taste
- 1 cup heavy cream
- 2 tablespoons all-purpose flour (optional, for thickening)

For the Gruyère Croutons:

- Baguette slices
- Gruyère cheese, grated

For Garnish:

- Fresh parsley, chopped

Instructions:

Saute Aromatics:

In a large pot, melt the butter over medium heat. Add chopped onions and sauté until softened, about 3-5 minutes. Add minced garlic and sauté for an additional 1-2 minutes until fragrant.

Cook Mushrooms:

Add the sliced mushrooms to the pot and cook until they release their moisture and become golden brown.

Season:

Season the mushrooms with salt, black pepper, and chopped thyme. Stir to combine.

Make Soup Base:

Pour in the vegetable or chicken broth, and bring the mixture to a simmer. Let it simmer for about 15-20 minutes, allowing the flavors to meld.

Blend the Soup:

Use an immersion blender to carefully blend the soup until smooth. Alternatively, transfer the soup in batches to a blender and blend until smooth. Be cautious, as hot liquids can splatter.

Thicken (Optional):

If you prefer a thicker soup, mix 2 tablespoons of all-purpose flour with a small amount of water to create a smooth paste. Stir the paste into the soup and simmer until the soup thickens.

Add Heavy Cream:

Pour in the heavy cream, stirring continuously. Let the soup simmer for an additional 5-10 minutes.

Season and Adjust:

Taste the soup and adjust the seasoning as needed. Add more salt and pepper if necessary.

Make Gruyère Croutons:

Preheat the oven broiler. Place baguette slices on a baking sheet and sprinkle grated Gruyère cheese on top. Broil until the cheese is melted and bubbly.

Serve:

Ladle the creamy mushroom soup into bowls. Top each serving with a Gruyère crouton.

Garnish:

> Garnish with chopped fresh parsley for a burst of color and freshness.

Enjoy:

> Serve immediately and enjoy the comforting and luxurious Creamy Mushroom Soup with Gruyère Croutons.

This Creamy Mushroom Soup with Gruyère Croutons is a delightful combination of earthy mushroom flavors and rich, creamy goodness. The cheesy croutons add a crunchy texture and an extra layer of savory delight to this comforting soup.

Corn Chowder with Cheddar and Bacon

Ingredients:

- 6 slices bacon, chopped
- 1 medium onion, diced
- 2 cloves garlic, minced
- 3 cups fresh or frozen corn kernels
- 1 large potato, peeled and diced
- 4 cups chicken or vegetable broth
- 1 teaspoon thyme, chopped
- 1/2 teaspoon smoked paprika
- Salt and black pepper to taste
- 1 cup sharp cheddar cheese, shredded
- 1 cup whole milk or heavy cream
- Fresh chives, chopped (for garnish)

Instructions:

Cook Bacon:

In a large pot, cook the chopped bacon over medium heat until it becomes crispy. Remove some bacon bits for garnish and leave the rest in the pot.

Saute Aromatics:

Add diced onions to the pot with the bacon and sauté until they become translucent. Add minced garlic and sauté for an additional minute.

Add Corn and Potato:

Stir in the corn kernels and diced potato. Cook for about 5 minutes to allow the vegetables to slightly soften.

Pour in Broth:

Pour in the chicken or vegetable broth, and add chopped thyme and smoked paprika. Season with salt and black pepper to taste.

Simmer:

Bring the mixture to a simmer and let it cook for 15-20 minutes or until the potatoes are tender.

Blend (Optional):

If desired, use an immersion blender to partially blend the soup to achieve a creamier consistency while leaving some chunks for texture.

Add Cheese and Milk:

Stir in the shredded cheddar cheese until melted. Pour in the whole milk or heavy cream, stirring continuously.

Adjust Seasoning:

Taste the chowder and adjust the seasoning with salt and black pepper if necessary.

Serve:

Ladle the corn chowder into bowls. Garnish with reserved crispy bacon bits and chopped fresh chives.

Enjoy:

Serve this flavorful Corn Chowder with Cheddar and Bacon hot, and savor the delicious combination of sweet corn, savory bacon, and creamy cheddar.

This hearty and comforting Corn Chowder with Cheddar and Bacon is a perfect dish for colder days. The smokiness of bacon, the sweetness of corn, and the richness of cheddar come together to create a bowl of soup that is both satisfying and flavorful.

Salads:
Caesar Salad with Homemade Dressing and Parmesan Crisps

Ingredients:

For the Caesar Dressing:

- 1/2 cup mayonnaise
- 2 tablespoons Dijon mustard
- 2 cloves garlic, minced
- 2 anchovy fillets, minced (optional)
- 2 tablespoons grated Parmesan cheese
- 1 tablespoon Worcestershire sauce
- 1 tablespoon red wine vinegar
- 1/2 cup extra-virgin olive oil
- Salt and black pepper to taste

For the Parmesan Crisps:

- 1 cup grated Parmesan cheese

For the Salad:

- Romaine lettuce, washed and torn into bite-sized pieces
- Croutons
- Additional grated Parmesan cheese for garnish

Instructions:

Prepare Caesar Dressing:

In a bowl, whisk together mayonnaise, Dijon mustard, minced garlic, anchovy fillets (if using), grated Parmesan cheese, Worcestershire sauce, and red wine vinegar.

Emulsify with Olive Oil:

While whisking continuously, slowly drizzle in the extra-virgin olive oil to emulsify the dressing. Continue whisking until the dressing is smooth and well combined.

Season:

Season the dressing with salt and black pepper to taste. Adjust the seasoning as needed.

Make Parmesan Crisps:

Preheat the oven to 375°F (190°C). Line a baking sheet with parchment paper. Place small mounds of grated Parmesan cheese on the parchment paper, spreading them out into thin rounds. Bake for 5-7 minutes or until the edges are golden brown and crispy. Allow them to cool before handling.

Assemble Salad:

In a large bowl, toss the torn Romaine lettuce with the Caesar dressing until well coated.

Add Croutons:

Add croutons to the salad and toss again to distribute them evenly.

Garnish with Parmesan:

Sprinkle additional grated Parmesan cheese over the salad.

Serve with Parmesan Crisps:

Arrange the Parmesan crisps on top of the Caesar salad for a crunchy and cheesy element.

Enjoy:

Serve the Caesar Salad with Homemade Dressing and Parmesan Crisps immediately, and enjoy this classic and flavorful salad!

This Caesar Salad with Homemade Dressing and Parmesan Crisps offers a perfect blend of crisp Romaine lettuce, creamy dressing, and crunchy Parmesan crisps. It's a delicious and satisfying dish that makes a great side or a light meal on its own.

Creamy Coleslaw with Buttermilk Dressing

Ingredients:

For the Coleslaw:

- 1 small green cabbage, shredded
- 2 large carrots, peeled and grated
- 1/2 small red onion, thinly sliced
- 1/2 cup fresh parsley, chopped (optional, for garnish)

For the Buttermilk Dressing:

- 1 cup mayonnaise
- 1/2 cup buttermilk
- 2 tablespoons apple cider vinegar
- 1 tablespoon Dijon mustard
- 2 tablespoons honey or sugar
- Salt and black pepper to taste

Instructions:

Prepare Vegetables:

Shred the green cabbage, grate the carrots, and thinly slice the red onion. Place them all in a large mixing bowl.

Make Buttermilk Dressing:

In a separate bowl, whisk together mayonnaise, buttermilk, apple cider vinegar, Dijon mustard, honey or sugar, salt, and black pepper. Whisk until the dressing is smooth and well combined.

Combine Dressing with Coleslaw:

Pour the buttermilk dressing over the shredded cabbage, grated carrots, and sliced red onion. Toss the coleslaw until the vegetables are evenly coated with the dressing.

Chill:

Cover the coleslaw and refrigerate for at least 1-2 hours before serving. This allows the flavors to meld, and the coleslaw becomes more flavorful.

Garnish (Optional):

Just before serving, garnish the coleslaw with fresh chopped parsley for a burst of color and freshness.

Adjust Seasoning:

Taste the coleslaw and adjust the seasoning if needed. You can add more salt, pepper, or a touch of honey for sweetness.

Serve:

Serve the Creamy Coleslaw with Buttermilk Dressing as a refreshing side dish for picnics, barbecues, or as a complement to sandwiches and burgers.

Enjoy:

Enjoy the cool, crisp, and creamy goodness of this classic coleslaw with the tangy kick of the buttermilk dressing!

This Creamy Coleslaw with Buttermilk Dressing is a crowd-pleaser with its refreshing crunch and delightful creaminess. The buttermilk dressing adds a tangy and slightly sweet flavor, making it the perfect side dish for a variety of meals.

Greek Salad with Feta and Kalamata Olives

Ingredients:

For the Salad:

- 1 large cucumber, diced
- 4 medium tomatoes, diced
- 1 red onion, thinly sliced
- 1 cup Kalamata olives, pitted
- 1 cup feta cheese, crumbled
- 1 cup cherry tomatoes, halved
- 1 green bell pepper, diced
- 1/2 cup fresh parsley, chopped
- 1/2 cup fresh mint leaves, chopped (optional)
- Salt and black pepper to taste

For the Dressing:

- 1/3 cup extra-virgin olive oil
- 3 tablespoons red wine vinegar
- 1 teaspoon dried oregano
- 1 clove garlic, minced
- Salt and black pepper to taste

Instructions:

Prepare Vegetables:

Dice the cucumber, tomatoes, and green bell pepper. Thinly slice the red onion. Halve the cherry tomatoes. Place them all in a large salad bowl.

Add Olives and Cheese:

Add Kalamata olives, crumbled feta cheese, and chopped fresh parsley to the bowl.

Make Dressing:

In a small bowl, whisk together extra-virgin olive oil, red wine vinegar, dried oregano, minced garlic, salt, and black pepper. Whisk until the dressing is well combined.

Combine Salad and Dressing:

Pour the dressing over the salad ingredients. Toss the salad gently to ensure the dressing coats all the vegetables evenly.

Season and Garnish:

Season the Greek salad with additional salt and black pepper to taste. Garnish with fresh mint leaves if desired.

Chill (Optional):

Refrigerate the Greek salad for about 30 minutes before serving to allow the flavors to meld and the salad to cool.

Serve:

Serve the Greek Salad with Feta and Kalamata Olives as a refreshing side dish or a light and healthy main course.

Enjoy:

Enjoy the vibrant and flavorful combination of crisp vegetables, briny olives, and creamy feta cheese in this classic Greek salad!

This Greek Salad is a perfect dish for summer or any time you crave a refreshing and wholesome salad. The combination of colorful vegetables, feta cheese, and olives, dressed in a zesty vinaigrette, makes for a delicious and satisfying meal.

Avocado and Goat Cheese Salad with Balsamic Vinaigrette

Ingredients:

For the Salad:

- 4 cups mixed salad greens (e.g., arugula, spinach, and mixed lettuces)
- 2 ripe avocados, sliced
- 1/2 cup cherry tomatoes, halved
- 1/4 cup red onion, thinly sliced
- 1/3 cup crumbled goat cheese
- 1/4 cup pine nuts, toasted
- Fresh basil leaves for garnish (optional)

For the Balsamic Vinaigrette:

- 1/4 cup extra-virgin olive oil
- 2 tablespoons balsamic vinegar
- 1 teaspoon Dijon mustard
- 1 clove garlic, minced
- Salt and black pepper to taste

Instructions:

Prepare Salad Greens:

In a large salad bowl, combine the mixed salad greens.

Add Avocado Slices:

Arrange the sliced avocados over the salad greens.

Sprinkle Tomatoes and Red Onion:

Sprinkle the halved cherry tomatoes and thinly sliced red onion over the salad.

Crumble Goat Cheese:

Crumble the goat cheese evenly over the salad.

Toast Pine Nuts:

In a dry skillet over medium heat, toast the pine nuts until they turn golden brown. Keep a close eye on them as they can burn quickly.

Add Toasted Pine Nuts:

Sprinkle the toasted pine nuts over the salad for added crunch.

Make Balsamic Vinaigrette:

In a small bowl, whisk together extra-virgin olive oil, balsamic vinegar, Dijon mustard, minced garlic, salt, and black pepper. Whisk until well combined.

Drizzle Dressing:

Drizzle the balsamic vinaigrette over the salad. Toss the salad gently to coat the ingredients with the dressing.

Garnish with Basil (Optional):

Garnish the salad with fresh basil leaves for a burst of flavor and aroma.

Serve:

Serve the Avocado and Goat Cheese Salad immediately as a refreshing and delightful appetizer or side dish.

Enjoy:

Enjoy the creamy avocado, tangy goat cheese, and the nutty crunch of pine nuts in this vibrant and flavorful salad!

This Avocado and Goat Cheese Salad with Balsamic Vinaigrette is a simple yet elegant dish that highlights the richness of avocado, the creaminess of goat cheese, and the sweet and tangy notes of balsamic vinaigrette. It's perfect for a light lunch or as a side to complement your main course.

Waldorf Salad with Blue Cheese Dressing

Ingredients:

For the Salad:

- 3 cups diced apples (use a mix of sweet and tart varieties)
- 1 cup celery, thinly sliced
- 1 cup red seedless grapes, halved
- 1 cup chopped walnuts
- 1/2 cup raisins or dried cranberries
- Fresh lettuce leaves for serving

For the Blue Cheese Dressing:

- 1/2 cup mayonnaise
- 1/4 cup sour cream
- 1/4 cup crumbled blue cheese
- 1 tablespoon apple cider vinegar
- 1 teaspoon Dijon mustard
- 1 clove garlic, minced
- Salt and black pepper to taste

Instructions:

Prepare Salad Ingredients:

Dice the apples, thinly slice the celery, halve the grapes, chop the walnuts, and gather the raisins or dried cranberries.

Make Blue Cheese Dressing:

In a bowl, whisk together mayonnaise, sour cream, crumbled blue cheese, apple cider vinegar, Dijon mustard, minced garlic, salt, and black pepper. Whisk until the dressing is smooth and well combined.

Assemble Waldorf Salad:

In a large mixing bowl, combine the diced apples, sliced celery, halved grapes, chopped walnuts, and raisins or dried cranberries.

Add Blue Cheese Dressing:

Pour the blue cheese dressing over the salad ingredients. Gently toss the salad until the ingredients are evenly coated with the dressing.

Chill (Optional):

Refrigerate the Waldorf Salad for about 30 minutes to allow the flavors to meld and the salad to cool.

Serve on Lettuce Leaves:

Arrange fresh lettuce leaves on a serving platter or individual plates. Spoon the Waldorf Salad onto the lettuce leaves.

Garnish (Optional):

Garnish the salad with additional crumbled blue cheese or a sprinkle of chopped walnuts for extra texture.

Serve:

Serve the Waldorf Salad with Blue Cheese Dressing as a refreshing side dish or a light and satisfying meal.

Enjoy:

Enjoy the delightful combination of sweet and crisp apples, crunchy celery, juicy grapes, and the richness of blue cheese in this classic Waldorf Salad!

This Waldorf Salad with Blue Cheese Dressing is a timeless dish that brings together a perfect balance of textures and flavors. It's a great choice for a light and satisfying meal or a refreshing side dish for a variety of occasions.

Main Courses:
Creamy Alfredo Pasta with Grilled Chicken

Ingredients:

For the Alfredo Sauce:

- 1/2 cup unsalted butter
- 2 cups heavy cream
- 2 cups grated Parmesan cheese
- Salt and black pepper to taste
- 1/2 teaspoon garlic powder (optional)

For the Pasta:

- 1 pound fettuccine or your preferred pasta
- Salt for boiling water

For the Grilled Chicken:

- 2 boneless, skinless chicken breasts
- 2 tablespoons olive oil
- 1 teaspoon garlic powder
- Salt and black pepper to taste
- 1 teaspoon dried Italian herbs (optional)

For Garnish:

- Fresh parsley, chopped
- Extra grated Parmesan cheese

Instructions:

Prepare Alfredo Sauce:

Melt Butter:

>In a saucepan over medium heat, melt the butter.

Add Cream:

Pour in the heavy cream and bring it to a gentle simmer.

Incorporate Parmesan:

Gradually whisk in the grated Parmesan cheese, stirring continuously until the cheese is fully melted and the sauce becomes creamy.

Season:

Season the Alfredo sauce with salt, black pepper, and garlic powder (if using). Adjust the seasoning according to your taste.

Keep Warm:

Reduce the heat to low, and let the Alfredo sauce simmer gently while you prepare the rest of the dish.

Grill Chicken:

Preheat Grill or Pan:

Preheat an outdoor grill or grill pan over medium-high heat.

Season Chicken:

Rub the chicken breasts with olive oil, garlic powder, salt, black pepper, and dried Italian herbs (if using).

Grill Chicken:

Grill the chicken breasts for about 6-8 minutes per side or until they reach an internal temperature of 165°F (74°C). Cooking times may vary depending on the thickness of the chicken.

Rest and Slice:

Allow the grilled chicken to rest for a few minutes before slicing it into thin strips.

Cook Pasta:

Boil Water:

Bring a large pot of salted water to a boil.

Cook Pasta:

Cook the fettuccine or your preferred pasta according to the package instructions until al dente.

Drain Pasta:

Drain the pasta, reserving a small amount of pasta water.

Assemble the Dish:

Combine Pasta and Sauce:

Add the drained pasta to the Alfredo sauce, tossing to coat the pasta evenly. If the sauce is too thick, you can add a bit of the reserved pasta water to reach your desired consistency.

Serve:

Divide the creamy Alfredo pasta among serving plates.

Top with Grilled Chicken:

Arrange the grilled chicken strips on top of the pasta.

Garnish:

Garnish with chopped fresh parsley and extra grated Parmesan cheese.

Enjoy:

Serve immediately, and enjoy this indulgent Creamy Alfredo Pasta with Grilled Chicken!

This Creamy Alfredo Pasta with Grilled Chicken is a delicious and satisfying dish that combines rich, creamy Alfredo sauce with perfectly grilled chicken. It's a classic comfort food recipe that's perfect for a special dinner or when you want to treat yourself to a decadent meal.

Four-Cheese Lasagna

Ingredients:

For the Meat Sauce:

- 1 pound ground beef or Italian sausage
- 1 onion, finely chopped
- 3 cloves garlic, minced
- 1 can (28 ounces) crushed tomatoes
- 1 can (14 ounces) diced tomatoes
- 2 cans (6 ounces each) tomato paste
- 1/4 cup red wine (optional)
- 2 teaspoons dried oregano
- 1 teaspoon dried basil
- Salt and black pepper to taste
- 1 tablespoon olive oil

For the Cheeses:

- 2 cups ricotta cheese
- 1 cup mozzarella cheese, shredded
- 1 cup Parmesan cheese, grated
- 1 cup provolone cheese, shredded

For Assembly:

- 9 lasagna noodles, cooked according to package instructions
- Fresh basil or parsley for garnish (optional)

Instructions:

Prepare the Meat Sauce:

Cook Ground Meat:

>In a large skillet or pot, heat olive oil over medium heat. Add the chopped onion and garlic, sautéing until softened. Add the ground beef or Italian sausage, breaking it apart and cooking until browned.

Add Tomatoes:

Stir in the crushed tomatoes, diced tomatoes, and tomato paste. Mix well.

Season:

Add red wine (if using), dried oregano, dried basil, salt, and black pepper. Stir to combine. Simmer the sauce over low heat for at least 30 minutes, allowing the flavors to meld.

Prepare the Cheeses:

Combine Cheeses:

In a bowl, combine ricotta cheese, mozzarella cheese, Parmesan cheese, and provolone cheese. Mix well.

Assemble the Lasagna:

Preheat Oven:

Preheat the oven to 375°F (190°C).

Layer the Lasagna:

In a 9x13-inch baking dish, spread a thin layer of the meat sauce on the bottom. Place three lasagna noodles over the sauce.

Cheese Layer:

Spread a portion of the cheese mixture over the noodles.

Repeat Layers:

Repeat the layering process, alternating between meat sauce, noodles, and cheese, until all ingredients are used. Ensure the top layer is meat sauce.

Cover and Bake:

Cover the baking dish with aluminum foil and bake in the preheated oven for 30 minutes.

Uncover and Bake:

Remove the foil and bake for an additional 15-20 minutes or until the lasagna is hot and bubbly, and the cheese is melted and golden.

Rest Before Serving:

Allow the lasagna to rest for 10-15 minutes before slicing. This helps the layers set and makes it easier to cut.

Garnish (Optional):

Garnish with fresh basil or parsley if desired.

Serve:

Slice and serve this delicious Four-Cheese Lasagna, and enjoy the cheesy layers of goodness!

This Four-Cheese Lasagna is a comforting and indulgent dish with layers of rich meat sauce and a blend of four cheeses. It's perfect for family dinners, special occasions, or anytime you crave a hearty and satisfying meal.

Beef Stroganoff with Sour Cream

Ingredients:

- 1.5 pounds beef sirloin or tenderloin, thinly sliced into strips
- Salt and black pepper to taste
- 2 tablespoons olive oil
- 1 onion, finely chopped
- 2 cloves garlic, minced
- 8 ounces mushrooms, sliced
- 2 tablespoons all-purpose flour
- 1 cup beef broth
- 2 tablespoons Worcestershire sauce
- 1 tablespoon Dijon mustard
- 1 cup sour cream
- 2 tablespoons chopped fresh parsley
- Egg noodles or rice for serving

Instructions:

Prepare Beef Strips:

Season the thinly sliced beef strips with salt and black pepper.

Sear Beef:

In a large skillet, heat olive oil over medium-high heat. Add the seasoned beef strips and sear until browned on all sides. Remove the beef from the skillet and set it aside.

Saute Onions and Garlic:

In the same skillet, add chopped onions and cook until they become translucent. Add minced garlic and cook for an additional 1-2 minutes.

Add Mushrooms:

Stir in the sliced mushrooms and cook until they release their moisture and become golden brown.

Make Roux:

Sprinkle flour over the mushroom mixture and stir to create a roux. Cook for 2-3 minutes to eliminate the raw flour taste.

Deglaze with Broth:

Gradually pour in the beef broth, Worcestershire sauce, and Dijon mustard, stirring continuously to avoid lumps. Bring the mixture to a simmer.

Reintroduce Beef:

Return the seared beef strips to the skillet, allowing them to cook in the flavorful sauce. Simmer for 5-7 minutes until the beef is cooked to your desired level of doneness.

Add Sour Cream:

Reduce the heat to low and stir in the sour cream. Heat the mixture gently, but avoid boiling to prevent curdling. Adjust the seasoning if needed.

Finish and Garnish:

Sprinkle chopped fresh parsley over the Beef Stroganoff for a burst of freshness.

Serve:

Serve the Beef Stroganoff with Sour Cream over egg noodles or rice.

Enjoy:

Enjoy this classic and comforting Beef Stroganoff with its creamy and savory flavors!

This Beef Stroganoff with Sour Cream is a timeless dish that combines tender beef strips with a rich and creamy sauce. It's a satisfying and flavorful meal that pairs perfectly with egg noodles or rice for a complete and comforting dining experience.

Spinach and Ricotta Stuffed Chicken Breast

Ingredients:

- 4 boneless, skinless chicken breasts
- Salt and black pepper to taste
- 2 cups fresh spinach, chopped
- 1 cup ricotta cheese
- 1/2 cup grated Parmesan cheese
- 2 cloves garlic, minced
- 1 teaspoon dried oregano
- 1 teaspoon dried basil
- 1 cup cherry tomatoes, halved
- Olive oil for drizzling
- Toothpicks or kitchen twine (optional)

Instructions:

Preheat Oven:

Preheat the oven to 375°F (190°C).

Prepare Chicken Breasts:

Lay each chicken breast flat on a cutting board. Use a sharp knife to butterfly each breast by making a horizontal cut along the side, being careful not to cut all the way through. Open the chicken breasts like a book.

Season and Tenderize:

Season the inside of each chicken breast with salt and black pepper. You can use a meat mallet to gently pound the breasts to an even thickness for easier stuffing.

Prepare Filling:

In a bowl, mix together chopped fresh spinach, ricotta cheese, grated Parmesan cheese, minced garlic, dried oregano, and dried basil.

Stuff Chicken Breasts:

Spoon the spinach and ricotta mixture onto one half of each butterflied chicken breast. Fold the other half over the filling, creating a stuffed chicken breast. Secure with toothpicks or kitchen twine if needed.

Season Outside:

Season the outside of each stuffed chicken breast with additional salt and black pepper.

Arrange in Baking Dish:

Place the stuffed chicken breasts in a baking dish. Scatter halved cherry tomatoes around the chicken.

Drizzle with Olive Oil:

Drizzle olive oil over the stuffed chicken breasts and tomatoes.

Bake:

Bake in the preheated oven for 25-30 minutes or until the chicken is cooked through and reaches an internal temperature of 165°F (74°C).

Broil (Optional):

If you want to add a golden crust, broil the stuffed chicken breasts for an additional 2-3 minutes, keeping a close eye to prevent burning.

Rest and Serve:

Allow the stuffed chicken breasts to rest for a few minutes before serving. Remove any toothpicks or twine before slicing.

Garnish (Optional):

Garnish with additional fresh herbs or grated Parmesan before serving.

Enjoy:

Serve the Spinach and Ricotta Stuffed Chicken Breast with the roasted cherry tomatoes, and enjoy this delicious and elegant dish!

This Spinach and Ricotta Stuffed Chicken Breast is a flavorful and impressive dish that brings together the richness of ricotta, the freshness of spinach, and the juicy tenderness of chicken. It's perfect for a special dinner or whenever you want to elevate your meal.

Creamy Shrimp Scampi over Linguine

Ingredients:

- 8 ounces linguine pasta
- 1 pound large shrimp, peeled and deveined
- Salt and black pepper to taste
- 3 tablespoons unsalted butter
- 3 tablespoons olive oil
- 4 cloves garlic, minced
- 1/2 teaspoon red pepper flakes (adjust to taste)
- 1 cup cherry tomatoes, halved
- 1/2 cup chicken broth
- 1/2 cup dry white wine
- 1 cup heavy cream
- Zest and juice of 1 lemon
- 1/2 cup grated Parmesan cheese
- Fresh parsley, chopped, for garnish

Instructions:

Cook Linguine:

Cook the linguine pasta according to the package instructions in a large pot of salted boiling water. Drain and set aside.

Season Shrimp:

Pat the shrimp dry and season with salt and black pepper.

Sauté Shrimp:

In a large skillet, heat 2 tablespoons of butter and 2 tablespoons of olive oil over medium-high heat. Add the shrimp and cook for 2-3 minutes per side until they turn pink. Remove the shrimp from the skillet and set aside.

Make Sauce:

In the same skillet, add the remaining 1 tablespoon of butter and 1 tablespoon of olive oil. Sauté minced garlic and red pepper flakes until fragrant.

Add Tomatoes:

Add the halved cherry tomatoes to the skillet and cook for 2-3 minutes until they start to soften.

Deglaze with Liquid:

Pour in the chicken broth and white wine, scraping any browned bits from the bottom of the skillet. Allow it to simmer for a couple of minutes.

Create Creamy Base:

Lower the heat and stir in the heavy cream, lemon zest, and lemon juice. Simmer for 2-3 minutes until the sauce thickens slightly.

Incorporate Parmesan:

Stir in the grated Parmesan cheese until it's fully melted into the sauce.

Return Shrimp:

Return the cooked shrimp to the skillet and toss them in the creamy sauce.

Combine with Linguine:

Add the cooked linguine to the skillet, tossing it with the creamy shrimp and sauce until everything is well coated.

Adjust Seasoning:

Taste and adjust the seasoning with salt and black pepper if needed.

Garnish and Serve:

Garnish with chopped fresh parsley and serve the Creamy Shrimp Scampi over Linguine immediately.

Enjoy:

Enjoy this luxurious and flavorful Creamy Shrimp Scampi over Linguine, a delightful dish that combines the richness of cream, the brightness of lemon, and the succulence of shrimp!

Vegetarian Options:
Three-Cheese Spinach and Mushroom Stuffed Peppers

Ingredients:

- 4 large bell peppers, halved and seeds removed
- 1 tablespoon olive oil
- 1 onion, finely chopped
- 2 cloves garlic, minced
- 8 ounces mushrooms, finely chopped
- 4 cups fresh spinach, chopped
- 1 cup ricotta cheese
- 1 cup mozzarella cheese, shredded
- 1/2 cup Parmesan cheese, grated
- Salt and black pepper to taste
- 1 teaspoon dried Italian herbs (optional)
- 1 can (14 ounces) crushed tomatoes
- Fresh basil or parsley for garnish

Instructions:

Preheat Oven:

Preheat the oven to 375°F (190°C).

Prepare Bell Peppers:

Cut the bell peppers in half lengthwise, removing the seeds and membranes. Place them in a baking dish.

Sauté Onion and Garlic:

In a large skillet, heat olive oil over medium heat. Add chopped onions and sauté until translucent. Add minced garlic and cook for an additional minute.

Cook Mushrooms and Spinach:

Add chopped mushrooms to the skillet and cook until they release their moisture. Stir in chopped spinach and cook until wilted. Drain any excess liquid.

Make Cheese Filling:

In a large bowl, combine ricotta cheese, mozzarella cheese, Parmesan cheese, salt, black pepper, and dried Italian herbs if using. Add the cooked mushroom and spinach mixture, mixing well.

Stuff Bell Peppers:

Fill each bell pepper half with the three-cheese spinach and mushroom mixture, pressing it down lightly.

Top with Crushed Tomatoes:

Pour crushed tomatoes over the stuffed peppers, ensuring they are well covered.

Bake:

Cover the baking dish with foil and bake in the preheated oven for 25-30 minutes, or until the peppers are tender.

Broil (Optional):

If desired, broil the stuffed peppers for an additional 2-3 minutes until the tops are golden brown.

Garnish and Serve:

Garnish the stuffed peppers with fresh basil or parsley.

Enjoy:

Serve these delicious Three-Cheese Spinach and Mushroom Stuffed Peppers as a flavorful and satisfying meal!

This Three-Cheese Spinach and Mushroom Stuffed Peppers recipe combines the goodness of ricotta, mozzarella, and Parmesan cheeses with the earthy flavors of mushrooms and spinach. It's a nutritious and tasty dish that makes for a wholesome meal or a delightful side.

Eggplant Parmesan with Mozzarella

Ingredients:

- 2 large eggplants, sliced into 1/2-inch rounds
- Salt for sweating eggplant
- 2 cups all-purpose flour
- 3 large eggs, beaten
- 2 cups breadcrumbs (Italian seasoned, if available)
- 1 cup grated Parmesan cheese
- Olive oil for frying
- 2 cups marinara sauce
- 2 cups shredded mozzarella cheese
- Fresh basil or parsley for garnish

Instructions:

Preheat Oven:

Preheat the oven to 375°F (190°C).

Slice and Sweat Eggplant:

Slice the eggplants into 1/2-inch rounds. Sprinkle salt on both sides of each slice and let them sit for about 30 minutes. This helps draw out excess moisture. Afterward, rinse the eggplant slices and pat them dry with paper towels.

Prepare Breading Station:

Set up a breading station with three shallow dishes: one with flour, one with beaten eggs, and one with a mixture of breadcrumbs and grated Parmesan cheese.

Bread Eggplant:

Dredge each eggplant slice in the flour, then dip it into the beaten eggs, and finally coat it with the breadcrumb-Parmesan mixture, pressing gently to adhere.

Fry Eggplant:

In a large skillet, heat olive oil over medium-high heat. Fry the breaded eggplant slices in batches until they are golden brown on both sides. Place them on a paper towel-lined plate to absorb excess oil.

Assemble in Baking Dish:

In a baking dish, spread a thin layer of marinara sauce. Arrange a layer of fried eggplant slices over the sauce. Sprinkle a portion of shredded mozzarella over the eggplant.

Repeat Layering:

Repeat the layering process until all the eggplant slices are used, finishing with a generous layer of mozzarella on top.

Bake:

Bake in the preheated oven for 25-30 minutes or until the cheese is melted and bubbly, and the edges are golden brown.

Broil (Optional):

If desired, broil for an additional 2-3 minutes until the cheese is golden and bubbly.

Garnish and Serve:

Garnish the Eggplant Parmesan with fresh basil or parsley.

Rest and Enjoy:

Allow the dish to rest for a few minutes before serving. Serve this Eggplant Parmesan with Mozzarella as a satisfying and flavorful vegetarian meal!

This Eggplant Parmesan with Mozzarella is a classic Italian dish that highlights the delicious combination of crispy fried eggplant, tangy marinara sauce, and gooey melted mozzarella cheese. It's a comforting and hearty dish that's perfect for a family dinner or a special occasion.

Creamy Pesto Pasta Primavera

Ingredients:

- 12 ounces penne or your favorite pasta
- 2 tablespoons olive oil
- 1 small red onion, thinly sliced
- 2 cloves garlic, minced
- 1 medium zucchini, thinly sliced
- 1 medium yellow squash, thinly sliced
- 1 cup cherry tomatoes, halved
- 1 cup broccoli florets
- 1 cup sliced bell peppers (mix of colors)
- Salt and black pepper to taste
- 1/2 cup pesto sauce (store-bought or homemade)
- 1 cup heavy cream
- 1/2 cup grated Parmesan cheese
- Fresh basil for garnish

Instructions:

Cook Pasta:

Cook the pasta according to the package instructions in a large pot of salted boiling water. Drain and set aside.

Prepare Vegetables:

In a large skillet, heat olive oil over medium heat. Add sliced red onion and minced garlic, sautéing until softened and fragrant.

Add Zucchini and Yellow Squash:

Add the thinly sliced zucchini and yellow squash to the skillet. Cook until the vegetables are tender-crisp.

Incorporate Cherry Tomatoes, Broccoli, and Bell Peppers:

Stir in the halved cherry tomatoes, broccoli florets, and sliced bell peppers. Cook for an additional 3-4 minutes until the vegetables are cooked but still vibrant.

Season:

Season the vegetable mixture with salt and black pepper to taste.

Add Pesto Sauce:

Add the pesto sauce to the skillet, stirring to coat the vegetables evenly.

Pour in Heavy Cream:

Pour in the heavy cream, stirring continuously. Allow the cream to simmer and thicken slightly.

Incorporate Parmesan Cheese:

Stir in the grated Parmesan cheese until it's fully melted into the creamy pesto sauce.

Combine with Cooked Pasta:

Add the cooked pasta to the skillet, tossing it with the creamy pesto and vegetable mixture until everything is well coated.

Adjust Seasoning:

Taste and adjust the seasoning if needed, adding more salt or pepper as desired.

Garnish and Serve:

Garnish the Creamy Pesto Pasta Primavera with fresh basil.

Enjoy:

Serve this delightful and vibrant Creamy Pesto Pasta Primavera immediately, and enjoy the flavors of fresh vegetables, creamy pesto, and perfectly cooked pasta!

This Creamy Pesto Pasta Primavera is a colorful and flavorful dish that celebrates the abundance of fresh vegetables. The combination of vibrant veggies, creamy pesto sauce, and Parmesan cheese creates a delicious and satisfying meal. Perfect for a quick and tasty weeknight dinner!

Cheesy Zucchini and Tomato Gratin

Ingredients:

- 4 medium-sized zucchini, thinly sliced
- 2 large tomatoes, thinly sliced
- 2 tablespoons olive oil
- 2 cloves garlic, minced
- 1 teaspoon dried thyme
- Salt and black pepper to taste
- 1 cup shredded mozzarella cheese
- 1/2 cup grated Parmesan cheese
- 1/2 cup breadcrumbs
- Fresh basil or parsley for garnish

Instructions:

Preheat Oven:

>Preheat the oven to 375°F (190°C).

Prepare Zucchini and Tomatoes:

>Thinly slice the zucchini and tomatoes.

Sauté Garlic and Zucchini:

>In a large skillet, heat olive oil over medium heat. Add minced garlic and sauté until fragrant. Add the thinly sliced zucchini to the skillet and cook until they are tender-crisp.

Season with Thyme:

>Season the zucchini with dried thyme, salt, and black pepper. Stir to combine.

Layer Zucchini and Tomatoes:

>In a greased baking dish, create alternating layers of sliced zucchini and tomatoes.

Cheese Layer:

Sprinkle shredded mozzarella and grated Parmesan cheese over each layer.

Repeat Layering:

Repeat the layering process until all the zucchini and tomatoes are used, finishing with a generous layer of cheese on top.

Top with Breadcrumbs:

Sprinkle breadcrumbs evenly over the top layer of cheese.

Bake:

Bake in the preheated oven for 25-30 minutes or until the cheese is melted and bubbly, and the top is golden brown.

Broil (Optional):

If desired, broil for an additional 2-3 minutes to achieve a golden crust on top.

Garnish:

Garnish the Cheesy Zucchini and Tomato Gratin with fresh basil or parsley.

Rest and Serve:

Allow the gratin to rest for a few minutes before serving.

Enjoy:

Serve this delicious Cheesy Zucchini and Tomato Gratin as a flavorful and satisfying side dish or a light vegetarian main course!

This Cheesy Zucchini and Tomato Gratin is a delightful and flavorful way to enjoy summer vegetables. The layers of zucchini and tomatoes, combined with melted mozzarella and Parmesan cheese, create a comforting and savory dish that's perfect for any occasion.

Spinach and Ricotta Stuffed Shells

Ingredients:

- 1 box (12 ounces) jumbo pasta shells
- 2 tablespoons olive oil
- 1 small onion, finely chopped
- 2 cloves garlic, minced
- 10 ounces fresh spinach, chopped
- 15 ounces ricotta cheese
- 1 cup shredded mozzarella cheese
- 1/2 cup grated Parmesan cheese
- 1 large egg, beaten
- 1 teaspoon dried oregano
- 1 teaspoon dried basil
- Salt and black pepper to taste
- 2 cups marinara sauce
- Fresh basil or parsley for garnish

Instructions:

Preheat Oven:

Preheat the oven to 375°F (190°C).

Cook Pasta Shells:

Cook the jumbo pasta shells according to the package instructions in a large pot of salted boiling water. Drain and set aside.

Prepare Spinach Mixture:

In a skillet, heat olive oil over medium heat. Add chopped onions and garlic, sautéing until softened. Add chopped fresh spinach and cook until wilted. Remove from heat and let it cool.

Make Ricotta Filling:

In a large bowl, combine ricotta cheese, shredded mozzarella, grated Parmesan, beaten egg, dried oregano, dried basil, salt, and black pepper. Add the cooled spinach mixture and mix until well combined.

Stuff Shells:

Using a spoon, carefully stuff each cooked jumbo shell with the spinach and ricotta mixture. Place the stuffed shells in a greased baking dish.

Top with Marinara Sauce:

Pour marinara sauce over the stuffed shells, ensuring they are well coated.

Bake:

Bake in the preheated oven for 25-30 minutes or until the shells are heated through and the cheese is melted and bubbly.

Broil (Optional):

If desired, broil for an additional 2-3 minutes to achieve a golden crust on top.

Garnish:

Garnish the Spinach and Ricotta Stuffed Shells with fresh basil or parsley.

Rest and Serve:

Allow the stuffed shells to rest for a few minutes before serving.

Enjoy:

Serve these delicious Spinach and Ricotta Stuffed Shells as a comforting and flavorful meal!

These Spinach and Ricotta Stuffed Shells are a classic Italian dish filled with creamy ricotta, vibrant spinach, and melted cheese. It's a comforting and satisfying meal that's perfect for family dinners or special occasions.

Side Dishes:

Creamy Mashed Potatoes with Butter and Cream

Ingredients:

- 4 large russet potatoes, peeled and quartered
- Salt for boiling water
- 1/2 cup unsalted butter, softened
- 1 cup heavy cream, warmed
- Salt and white pepper to taste
- Chopped fresh chives or parsley for garnish (optional)

Instructions:

Boil Potatoes:

> Place the peeled and quartered potatoes in a large pot of salted boiling water. Cook until the potatoes are fork-tender, about 15-20 minutes.

Drain Potatoes:

> Drain the cooked potatoes thoroughly.

Mash Potatoes:

> Use a potato masher or a ricer to mash the potatoes until smooth. Ensure there are no lumps.

Add Butter:

> Add softened butter to the mashed potatoes. Mix well until the butter is fully incorporated.

Warm Heavy Cream:

> Warm the heavy cream either in a saucepan or the microwave until it's hot but not boiling.

Pour Cream Over Potatoes:

Gradually pour the warm heavy cream over the mashed potatoes while mixing continuously. Continue to mix until the cream is fully incorporated and the mashed potatoes reach your desired consistency.

Season:

Season the creamy mashed potatoes with salt and white pepper to taste. Adjust the seasoning according to your preference.

Garnish (Optional):

If desired, garnish the creamy mashed potatoes with chopped fresh chives or parsley for a burst of freshness.

Serve Warm:

Serve the Creamy Mashed Potatoes with Butter and Cream immediately while they are warm.

Enjoy:

Enjoy these velvety, rich, and Creamy Mashed Potatoes as a comforting side dish to complement your favorite main courses!

These Creamy Mashed Potatoes with Butter and Cream are a classic and indulgent side dish that pairs well with various mains. The combination of butter and cream creates a silky texture, making these mashed potatoes incredibly flavorful and satisfying. Perfect for holiday dinners, family gatherings, or whenever you crave a comforting side dish.

Grilled Asparagus with Parmesan Cheese

Ingredients:

- 1 bunch fresh asparagus spears, woody ends trimmed
- 2 tablespoons olive oil
- Salt and black pepper to taste
- 1/4 cup grated Parmesan cheese
- Lemon wedges for serving (optional)

Instructions:

Preheat Grill:

Preheat your grill to medium-high heat.

Prepare Asparagus:

Trim the woody ends from the asparagus spears. If the spears are thick, you can peel the lower portion for a more even cooking.

Coat with Olive Oil:

In a large bowl, toss the asparagus spears with olive oil, ensuring they are evenly coated.

Season:

Season the asparagus with salt and black pepper to taste. Toss again to distribute the seasoning.

Grill Asparagus:

Place the asparagus spears on the preheated grill. Grill for 3-5 minutes, turning occasionally, until they are tender and have grill marks.

Sprinkle with Parmesan:

During the last minute of grilling, sprinkle the grated Parmesan cheese over the asparagus. Close the grill lid for a short time to allow the cheese to melt slightly.

Serve:

Remove the grilled asparagus from the grill and transfer them to a serving platter. Squeeze lemon wedges over the asparagus for a bright, citrusy finish if desired.

Enjoy:

Serve the Grilled Asparagus with Parmesan Cheese as a delightful side dish. The combination of smoky grilled asparagus and the savory kick of Parmesan makes for a simple yet flavorful addition to your meal.

Creamed Spinach with Nutmeg

Ingredients:

- 1 pound fresh spinach, washed and stems removed
- 2 tablespoons unsalted butter
- 2 tablespoons all-purpose flour
- 1 cup whole milk
- 1/4 teaspoon ground nutmeg
- Salt and black pepper to taste
- 1/4 cup grated Parmesan cheese (optional)
- Lemon wedges for serving (optional)

Instructions:

Blanch Spinach:

In a large pot of boiling salted water, blanch the spinach for 1-2 minutes until wilted. Drain and immediately transfer to a bowl of ice water to stop the cooking process. Drain again and squeeze out excess water. Chop the blanched spinach finely.

Make Roux:

In a medium saucepan, melt the butter over medium heat. Add the flour and whisk continuously to create a smooth roux. Cook for 1-2 minutes, being careful not to let it brown.

Add Milk:

Gradually add the milk to the roux, whisking constantly to avoid lumps. Continue cooking and whisking until the mixture thickens.

Season with Nutmeg:

Add ground nutmeg to the creamy sauce. Nutmeg adds a warm and aromatic flavor that complements the spinach well. Season with salt and black pepper to taste.

Incorporate Spinach:

Stir in the chopped blanched spinach, ensuring it is well coated with the creamy sauce. Cook for an additional 2-3 minutes until heated through.

Optional Parmesan Cheese:

For an extra layer of flavor, you can add grated Parmesan cheese to the creamed spinach. Stir it in until melted and well combined.

Adjust Seasoning:

Taste the creamed spinach and adjust the seasoning if needed, adding more salt, pepper, or nutmeg to suit your taste.

Serve:

Transfer the Creamed Spinach with Nutmeg to a serving dish. Optionally, squeeze a bit of fresh lemon juice over the top for a burst of citrusy brightness.

Enjoy:

Serve the creamed spinach as a delicious and comforting side dish, perfect for accompanying a variety of main courses.

This Creamed Spinach with Nutmeg is a classic side dish that combines the richness of cream, the earthy flavor of spinach, and the warm aroma of nutmeg. It's a versatile accompaniment that pairs well with roasted meats, grilled chicken, or even as a topping for baked potatoes.

Macaroni and Cheese with a Crispy Bread Crumb Topping

Ingredients:

For Macaroni and Cheese:

- 8 ounces elbow macaroni or your favorite pasta
- 1/4 cup unsalted butter
- 1/4 cup all-purpose flour
- 1/2 teaspoon mustard powder
- 1/4 teaspoon cayenne pepper (optional)
- 3 cups whole milk
- 3 cups shredded sharp cheddar cheese
- 1 cup shredded mozzarella cheese
- Salt and black pepper to taste

For Crispy Bread Crumb Topping:

- 1 cup Panko bread crumbs
- 2 tablespoons unsalted butter, melted
- 1/4 cup grated Parmesan cheese
- 1 teaspoon dried thyme (optional)
- Salt and black pepper to taste

Instructions:

Preheat Oven:

Preheat your oven to 375°F (190°C).

Cook Pasta:

Cook the elbow macaroni or pasta according to the package instructions in a large pot of salted boiling water. Drain and set aside.

Make Cheese Sauce:

In a large saucepan, melt 1/4 cup of butter over medium heat. Stir in the flour, mustard powder, and cayenne pepper (if using) to create a roux. Cook for 1-2 minutes.

Add Milk:

Gradually whisk in the whole milk, ensuring there are no lumps. Continue cooking and whisking until the mixture thickens.

Incorporate Cheese:

Reduce heat to low, and stir in the shredded cheddar and mozzarella cheeses. Keep stirring until the cheese is fully melted and the sauce is smooth. Season with salt and black pepper to taste.

Combine with Pasta:

Add the cooked pasta to the cheese sauce, stirring until the pasta is well coated.

Prepare Topping:

In a small bowl, mix together the Panko bread crumbs, melted butter, grated Parmesan cheese, dried thyme (if using), salt, and black pepper.

Assemble and Bake:

Transfer the macaroni and cheese mixture to a greased baking dish. Sprinkle the Panko bread crumb topping evenly over the pasta.

Bake in Oven:

Bake in the preheated oven for 20-25 minutes or until the top is golden brown and the cheese is bubbly.

Serve:

Remove from the oven and let it rest for a few minutes. Serve the Macaroni and Cheese with a Crispy Bread Crumb Topping as a comforting and cheesy delight!

This Macaroni and Cheese with a Crispy Bread Crumb Topping brings together the creamy goodness of a classic mac and cheese with a crunchy and flavorful topping. It's a perfect dish for family gatherings, potlucks, or whenever you're craving a comforting and indulgent meal.

Scalloped Potatoes with Gruyère and Thyme

Ingredients:

- 2 pounds Yukon Gold potatoes, peeled and thinly sliced
- 2 tablespoons unsalted butter
- 2 tablespoons all-purpose flour
- 2 cups whole milk, warmed
- 1 1/2 cups shredded Gruyère cheese
- 2 cloves garlic, minced
- 1 teaspoon fresh thyme leaves, plus extra for garnish
- Salt and black pepper to taste
- 1/4 cup grated Parmesan cheese (optional)
- Chopped fresh parsley for garnish (optional)

Instructions:

Preheat Oven:

    Preheat your oven to 375°F (190°C).

Prepare Potatoes:

    Peel and thinly slice the Yukon Gold potatoes using a mandoline or a sharp knife.

Make Cheese Sauce:

    In a medium saucepan, melt the butter over medium heat. Add the flour and whisk continuously to create a smooth roux. Cook for 1-2 minutes, being careful not to let it brown.

Add Warm Milk:

    Gradually pour in the warm whole milk, whisking constantly to avoid lumps. Continue cooking and whisking until the mixture thickens.

Incorporate Cheese:

    Stir in the shredded Gruyère cheese until fully melted and the sauce is smooth. Season with salt and black pepper to taste.

Add Garlic and Thyme:

Add minced garlic and fresh thyme leaves to the cheese sauce, stirring to incorporate. The garlic and thyme add aromatic flavors to the dish.

Layer Potatoes:

In a greased baking dish, create layers of sliced potatoes, pouring some of the cheese sauce over each layer. Repeat until all potatoes are used, finishing with a layer of cheese sauce on top.

Optional Parmesan Topping:

Sprinkle grated Parmesan cheese over the top for an additional layer of flavor.

Bake in Oven:

Bake in the preheated oven for 45-50 minutes or until the potatoes are tender, and the top is golden brown and bubbly.

Rest Before Serving:

Allow the Scalloped Potatoes with Gruyère and Thyme to rest for a few minutes before serving.

Garnish and Serve:

Garnish with extra fresh thyme leaves and chopped parsley if desired.

Enjoy:

Serve this decadent and flavorful Scalloped Potatoes with Gruyère and Thyme as a delightful side dish for special occasions or as a comforting addition to your meals!

These Scalloped Potatoes are elevated with the nutty flavor of Gruyère cheese and the aromatic essence of fresh thyme. Creamy and rich, this dish is perfect for holiday dinners or any time you want a comforting and indulgent side dish.

Breads and Rolls:
Cheesy Garlic Breadsticks

Ingredients:

For the Dough:

- 1 1/2 cups warm water (about 110°F or 43°C)
- 2 teaspoons sugar
- 2 1/4 teaspoons active dry yeast (1 packet)
- 4 cups all-purpose flour
- 1 1/2 teaspoons salt
- 2 tablespoons olive oil

For the Garlic Butter:

- 1/2 cup unsalted butter, melted
- 3 cloves garlic, minced
- 2 tablespoons fresh parsley, finely chopped (optional)
- Salt to taste

For the Cheese Topping:

- 1 1/2 cups shredded mozzarella cheese
- 1/2 cup grated Parmesan cheese

Instructions:

Activate Yeast:

In a bowl, combine warm water and sugar. Sprinkle active dry yeast over the water and let it sit for about 5 minutes, or until it becomes foamy.

Prepare Dough:

In a large mixing bowl, combine flour and salt. Make a well in the center and add the activated yeast mixture and olive oil. Mix until a dough forms.

Knead Dough:

Turn the dough onto a floured surface and knead for about 5-7 minutes, or until it becomes smooth and elastic. Place the dough in a lightly oiled bowl, cover with a damp cloth, and let it rise in a warm place for about 1 hour, or until it doubles in size.

Preheat Oven:

Preheat your oven to 400°F (200°C).

Roll Out Dough:

Once the dough has risen, punch it down and roll it out on a floured surface into a rectangle, about 12x18 inches.

Prepare Garlic Butter:

In a small bowl, mix together melted butter, minced garlic, chopped parsley (if using), and salt to taste.

Add Garlic Butter and Cheese:

Brush the rolled-out dough with the garlic butter mixture. Sprinkle shredded mozzarella and grated Parmesan evenly over the dough.

Fold and Cut:

Fold the dough in half, covering the cheese, and gently press to seal. Cut the dough into strips, creating breadsticks.

Twist and Place on Baking Sheet:

Twist each strip and place the twisted breadsticks on a parchment-lined baking sheet.

Bake:

Bake in the preheated oven for 12-15 minutes or until the breadsticks are golden brown and the cheese is melted.

Serve:

> Remove from the oven and serve the Cheesy Garlic Breadsticks warm. Enjoy as an appetizer or alongside your favorite pasta dish!

These Cheesy Garlic Breadsticks are a delicious combination of soft, flavorful dough, garlicky butter, and melted cheese. They make a fantastic accompaniment to pasta dishes, soups, or as a tasty snack on their own. Enjoy the irresistible aroma and cheesy goodness!

Cheddar and Herb Biscuits

Ingredients:

- 2 cups all-purpose flour
- 1 tablespoon baking powder
- 1/2 teaspoon baking soda
- 1/2 teaspoon salt
- 1/2 cup unsalted butter, cold and cut into small cubes
- 1 cup sharp cheddar cheese, shredded
- 1 tablespoon fresh herbs (such as chives, parsley, or thyme), finely chopped
- 3/4 cup buttermilk
- 1 tablespoon honey (optional, for a touch of sweetness)

Instructions:

Preheat Oven:

Preheat your oven to 425°F (220°C). Line a baking sheet with parchment paper.

Prepare Dry Ingredients:

In a large bowl, whisk together the all-purpose flour, baking powder, baking soda, and salt.

Incorporate Butter:

Add the cold, cubed butter to the dry ingredients. Use a pastry cutter or your fingers to work the butter into the flour until the mixture resembles coarse crumbs.

Add Cheese and Herbs:

Mix in the shredded cheddar cheese and finely chopped fresh herbs, ensuring they are evenly distributed throughout the mixture.

Combine with Buttermilk:

Pour in the buttermilk (and honey if using), stirring until just combined. Be careful not to overmix; the dough should be slightly sticky.

Shape and Cut Biscuits:

> Turn the dough out onto a floured surface and gently pat it into a rectangle, about 1-inch thick. Using a biscuit cutter or a round glass, cut out biscuits and place them on the prepared baking sheet.

Bake:

> Bake in the preheated oven for 12-15 minutes or until the biscuits are golden brown on top.

Serve Warm:

> Allow the Cheddar and Herb Biscuits to cool slightly before serving. They are best enjoyed warm.

Optional: Brush with Butter (Optional):

> For an extra indulgence, you can brush the warm biscuits with melted butter before serving.

Enjoy:

> Serve these delightful Cheddar and Herb Biscuits alongside soups, stews, or as a tasty accompaniment to any meal. Enjoy the cheesy goodness and aromatic herbs in every bite!

These Cheddar and Herb Biscuits are a savory delight with a perfect balance of cheesy goodness and fresh herbs. They are quick and easy to make, making them a wonderful addition to any meal or a delicious snack on their own.

Cream Cheese Danish Pastry

Ingredients:

For the Pastry:

- 2 sheets puff pastry, thawed if frozen
- 8 ounces cream cheese, softened
- 1/2 cup granulated sugar
- 1 teaspoon vanilla extract
- 1 large egg (for egg wash)

For the Glaze:

- 1 cup powdered sugar
- 2 tablespoons milk
- 1/2 teaspoon vanilla extract

Instructions:

Preheat Oven:

Preheat your oven to 375°F (190°C). Line a baking sheet with parchment paper.

Prepare Cream Cheese Filling:

In a bowl, combine softened cream cheese, granulated sugar, and vanilla extract. Mix until smooth and well combined.

Roll Out Puff Pastry:

Roll out each sheet of puff pastry on a lightly floured surface. Cut each sheet into squares or rectangles, depending on your preference.

Add Cream Cheese Filling:

Spoon a generous dollop of the cream cheese mixture onto the center of each puff pastry square.

Fold and Seal:

Fold the corners of the pastry over the cream cheese filling, forming a pinwheel or envelope shape. Press the edges to seal.

Egg Wash:

Beat the egg and brush it over the top of each pastry for a golden finish.

Bake:

Place the filled pastries on the prepared baking sheet and bake in the preheated oven for 15-20 minutes or until the pastries are puffed and golden brown.

Make Glaze:

While the pastries are baking, prepare the glaze by mixing powdered sugar, milk, and vanilla extract in a bowl until smooth.

Glaze the Pastries:

Once the pastries are out of the oven and slightly cooled, drizzle the glaze over the top.

Serve:

Allow the Cream Cheese Danish Pastries to cool completely before serving. Enjoy these delightful pastries with a cup of coffee or tea!

These Cream Cheese Danish Pastries are a delightful treat with flaky puff pastry and a rich cream cheese filling. The sweet glaze on top adds an extra layer of flavor. Perfect for breakfast, brunch, or as a sweet indulgence with your favorite hot beverage!

Gouda and Chive Scones

Ingredients:

- 2 cups all-purpose flour
- 1 tablespoon baking powder
- 1/2 teaspoon salt
- 1/2 cup unsalted butter, cold and cut into small cubes
- 1 cup Gouda cheese, grated
- 2 tablespoons fresh chives, finely chopped
- 2/3 cup buttermilk
- 1 large egg (for egg wash)
- Extra flour for dusting

Instructions:

Preheat Oven:

Preheat your oven to 400°F (200°C). Line a baking sheet with parchment paper.

Prepare Dry Ingredients:

In a large bowl, whisk together the all-purpose flour, baking powder, and salt.

Incorporate Butter:

Add the cold, cubed butter to the dry ingredients. Use a pastry cutter or your fingers to work the butter into the flour until the mixture resembles coarse crumbs.

Add Gouda and Chives:

Mix in the grated Gouda cheese and finely chopped fresh chives, ensuring they are evenly distributed throughout the mixture.

Combine with Buttermilk:

Pour in the buttermilk, stirring until just combined. Be careful not to overmix; the dough should be slightly sticky.

Shape and Cut Scones:

Turn the dough out onto a floured surface and gently pat it into a circle, about 1-inch thick. Use a round biscuit cutter to cut out scones. Place them on the prepared baking sheet.

Egg Wash:

Beat the egg and brush it over the top of each scone for a golden finish.

Bake:

Bake in the preheated oven for 15-18 minutes or until the scones are golden brown.

Cool:

Allow the Gouda and Chive Scones to cool slightly before serving.

Serve:

Serve these flavorful scones warm, either on their own or with a dollop of butter. They make a delicious addition to brunch or tea time!

These Gouda and Chive Scones are a delightful combination of rich Gouda cheese and the freshness of chives. The flaky texture and savory flavors make them a perfect choice for a savory breakfast or brunch treat. Enjoy these scones fresh out of the oven!

Feta and Sun-Dried Tomato Pull-Apart Bread

Ingredients:

For the Bread Dough:

- 3 1/2 cups all-purpose flour
- 1 tablespoon sugar
- 1 teaspoon salt
- 1 1/4 cups warm milk (about 110°F or 43°C)
- 2 teaspoons active dry yeast
- 1/4 cup unsalted butter, melted

For the Filling:

- 1 cup crumbled feta cheese
- 1/2 cup sun-dried tomatoes, chopped
- 2 tablespoons fresh basil, chopped
- 2 tablespoons olive oil

For the Garlic Butter Glaze:

- 1/4 cup unsalted butter, melted
- 2 cloves garlic, minced
- 1 tablespoon fresh parsley, chopped
- Salt to taste

Instructions:

Prepare the Dough:

Activate Yeast:

In a bowl, combine warm milk and sugar. Sprinkle active dry yeast over the mixture, and let it sit for about 5 minutes or until it becomes foamy.

Mix Dry Ingredients:

In a large mixing bowl, whisk together the flour and salt.

Combine Ingredients:

Add the activated yeast mixture and melted butter to the dry ingredients. Mix until a dough forms.

Knead Dough:

Turn the dough onto a floured surface and knead for about 8-10 minutes, or until it becomes smooth and elastic.

First Rise:

Place the kneaded dough in a greased bowl, cover it with a damp cloth, and let it rise in a warm place for about 1 hour or until it doubles in size.

Assemble the Pull-Apart Bread:

Preheat Oven:

Preheat your oven to 350°F (175°C). Grease a bundt pan.

Roll Out Dough:

Roll out the risen dough on a floured surface into a large rectangle.

Add Filling:

In a bowl, mix together crumbled feta, chopped sun-dried tomatoes, fresh basil, and olive oil. Spread this mixture evenly over the rolled-out dough.

Roll and Cut:

Roll the dough into a log and slice it into small rounds. Arrange the rounds in the greased bundt pan.

Second Rise:

Cover the pan with a damp cloth and let it rise for an additional 20-30 minutes.

Make the Garlic Butter Glaze:

Prepare Glaze:

In a small bowl, mix together melted butter, minced garlic, chopped parsley, and salt to taste.

Bake and Glaze:

Bake:

Bake the Feta and Sun-Dried Tomato Pull-Apart Bread in the preheated oven for 25-30 minutes or until golden brown.

Glaze:

Remove from the oven and immediately brush the garlic butter glaze over the bread.

Serve:

Allow the bread to cool slightly before removing it from the pan. Serve the Feta and Sun-Dried Tomato Pull-Apart Bread warm. Enjoy pulling apart the delicious, cheesy, and flavorful layers!

This Feta and Sun-Dried Tomato Pull-Apart Bread is a crowd-pleasing appetizer or side dish with layers of savory goodness. The combination of feta, sun-dried tomatoes, and garlic butter makes it a deliciously irresistible treat. Perfect for sharing at gatherings or as a special addition to your meals.